garden**M**ania

philip de bay & james bolton

garden Mania

the ardent gardener's compendium of design & decoration

with a preface by monty don

CLARKSON POTTER / PUBLISHERS
New York

On the cover A Dutch formal garden, *c.* 1700.

Half title A French fashion plate of 1799 by Vernet: a lady of the Directoire sporting a revolutionary floral bonnet.

Frontispiece A view from the terrace of the nineteenth-century Italianate gardens at Shrubland, Suffolk, England.

This page A French Baroque design by Jean Le Pautre for a nymph supporting a flowering urn.

Published by Clarkson Potter/Publishers, New York, New York. Member of the Crown Publishing Group.

Random House Inc. New York, Toronto, London, Sydney, Auckland

www.randomhouse.com

CLARKSON N. POTTER is a trademark and POTTER and colophon are registered trademarks of Random House, Inc.

Originally published in Great Britain by Thames & Hudson Ltd., London, in 2000.

Library of Congress Cataloging-in-Publication Data available upon request from the publisher.

ISBN 0-609-80728-5

10 9 8 7 6 5 4 3 2 1

First American Edition

Printed and bound in China

Contents

Preface by Monty Don

Gardening in the twenty-first century is by and large an urban activity and has therefore become most people's closest contact with 'nature'. Enormous store is set by the amount of wildlife that can be induced to share our small back-gardens. Yet it is a measure of how far modern man lives from the influence of the natural world that he looks for it in his garden. After all, from the first, every garden has been a manifestation of man's need to control and tame nature. The garden of Eden was fashioned from the first in man's image. The fall from grace was a measure of bad gardening as much as eye-popping sexual awareness. Can fallen man make a perfect garden? Certainly, as this book shows, we have been trying for a very long time.

Looking through the collection of illustrations that Philip de Bay has gathered for this book, I am struck by how ill at ease most of the humans are, parading around their highly ornate and structured defiance of the forces of nature around them. In the portraits of formal gardens human activity is restricted to a slow perambulation. Any evidence of the frenzied activity of the teams of gardeners needed to maintain that static image is unusual, although they do exist. My favourite is on pages 372–73, where workers at the Prince of Lichtenstein's garden near Vienna are bringing out orange trees. The overturned empty barrel and dumped roller and rake fire the formal array of topiary and tender greens with an utterly modern and familiar gardening reality. The main exceptions to this rule, as on pages 286–87, are pictures of human activity with the gardens merely a backdrop, created like a stage set for a masque. This, I think, is the clue to the enduring power of gardening: at its core it is an entirely human activity. After all, nature hardly needs us to grow its own. All the devices and conceits that this book so wonderfully illustrates are part of the instinctive human desire to tame and reclaim their domestic space away from nature rather than to share it with the natural world.

And yet what makes gardening in all its forms so richly satisfying is the way that, out of the constant conflict of man's desire to control and order his world and the inherent uncontrollability of the natural world around him, comes a genuine creative expression. Making a garden has always been one of the grandest and yet most available of all art forms. This book is a chronicle of the desire not to repress nature but to make something of it in man's own image, and there is something heroic about the vanity and folly of this. As a result, as one who is self-confessedly mad about gardening, I find *Garden Mania* a wonderfully sane celebration of the essential vein of humanity that runs right through the heart of every garden.

Page 6 An eighteenth-century fashion plate from the *Galérie des Modes*, showing trellis and topiary.

Introduction Garden Mania

Gardens have been a source of delight, desire and pleasure for centuries. The urge to control and to enjoy nature, to create an earthly paradise, through the designs, the ornaments, the flowers and the shrubs which combine to make up the garden is one of the most delightful of human manias. Over the centuries this obsession with horticultural delight has taken many forms and expressions, from the architectural delights of the Baroque gardens of Italy, via the vistas and parterres of Versailles, to the herbaceous borders of village England. It has also been recorded in the prints and albums of large-scale and small-scale garden designs from which the hundreds of fascinating images reproduced in this book are drawn, to create a feast for the practising and the armchair gardener.

Here are the fruits of expert plantsmanship: parterres, hedges, mazes and topiary. Here, too, are the architectural forms of weird and wonderful structures in wood, stone and metal. Temples, pavilions, conservatories, orangeries, follies, mausoleums and ruins are countered on the human scale by statuary, urns and every style of wooden structure – Gothick, Classical, Moorish and Oriental. Ingenious swings and helter-skelters, pigeon-houses, aviaries and menageries extend the delights of this place of amusement and surprise – the garden.

Gardens have always been made for enjoyment, whether aesthetic or as the providers of comestibles. They are distractions from the realities of everyday life and the outside world. From the earliest Persian garden, turned resolutely in on itself, to the modest present-day suburban garden, their purpose is to soothe, refresh and invigorate. In Ancient Egypt, the Pharaoh was rowed across garden pools by girls clad only in gold nets. In Sicily, Archimedes created a floating garden with shady walks and ornamental water. The Emperor Hadrian constructed a sumptuous dining-room at his villa at Tivoli, where his guests reclined and feasted amid cascades and other water features. In medieval England, gardens were for lovers, who reclined on turf benches and bathed together in pools under elaborate fountains.

The garden is a place of display, nurtured carefully by the obsessive gardener: the colours of flowers, the sparkling of water in fountains and cascades, the gleam of white marble. The ear is delighted by the trickle of a rill or the calling and singing of birds in the trees or nearby aviary. And to intensify the gratification of the senses, what better than to array this paradise regained with ingenious ornaments to amuse and beguile the visitor and guest?

Display and delight were undoubtedly uppermost in the minds of the designers and architects of the sixteenth- and seventeenth-century gardens of Italy, lavishly ornamental in deliberate imitation of the glories of Ancient Rome. The gardens at the Villa d'Este, for instance, designed in the 1560s, harnessed the waters of the river Aniene to provide a profusion of fountains and pools, water staircases and cascades. Statues were taken from the ruins of Hadrian's Villa nearby to adorn the garden and to give additional significance to the lavish display. Images of Hercules, the mythical ancestor of the d'Este family, featured prominently. In places, visitors were offered a moral choice: the path of virtue, represented by the grotto of Diana, or the path of vice in the form of the grotto of Venus. Ingenious hydraulic devices caused mechanical birds to sing or organs to play, or set off jets to soak the unwary guest.

Above Detail of bird from an early eighteenth-century print.

As fashion-conscious Europe turned to French styles of architecture and decoration in the mid seventeenth century, so France became the centre of garden mania in the grand style during the same period. At Vaux-le-Vicomte in 1653, Louis XIV's minister, Nicolas Fouquet, employed Le Nôtre to create a colossal garden of regal magnificence. Fouquet invited the king to a spectacular fête in the garden, which Louis described as 'insolent and audacious'. Fouquet's fate was sealed; he was imprisoned, and the plants and ornaments of his sumptuous gardens were transferred to Versailles. Louis also retained the services of Le Nôtre. At Versailles, ornament was deeply political, symbolizing the glory of the Sun King and reflecting the power and prestige of France.

Versailles mania spread across Europe. No prince or princeling worthy of his title was content until he too had remodelled his garden in imitation of Le Nôtre. In Vienna, the Hapsburgs rebuilt Schönbrunn, which like Versailles had originally been a hunting-lodge, deliberately to rival the French original. Parterres stretch into the distance and high walls of clipped trees divide the garden into squares and rectangles. In Germany, Schwetzingen boasted a vast circular parterre with curved trellis arches.

Garden mania is bipartite; it thrives on the interplay and alternation of the formal and informal. The fountains and parterres, steps and terraces, bosquets and arbours all so fashionable in the late seventeenth century and in the early eighteenth were bound to provoke a reaction. With political power shifting northwards after the death of Louis XIV, so the revolt against formality and classicism first began in England.

Decoration returned in the early years of the nineteenth century; terraces with balustrades of stone or wrought-iron and even fountains reappeared. Of the many varied styles which proliferated, none was as popular as the 'Italianate'. Shrubland Park, where the garden was laid out by the eminent Victorian

Above Detail of horned beetle from an early eighteenth-century print.

architect Sir Charles Barry, was dominated by an enormous staircase of 137 steps which carried the visitor down the escarpment to the lower terrace. In the United States, Edith Wharton's books on Italian villas created a craze for this style among the newly rich, determined to display their wealth. The Villa Vizcaya in Florida, partly based on the Villa Lante, is a remarkable reproduction of a sixteenth-century Italian garden; among the parterres and *allées* of evergreen oak, a stone boat floats in the sea just off-shore from a formal terrace. Dumbarton Oaks in Washington D.C., by the designer Beatrix Farrand, looks like an Italian design out of the Arts and Crafts Movement!

Technological advances during the nineteenth century gave the ardent horticulturalist a much wider range of materials with which to ornament a garden. A Mrs. Coade of Lambeth invented a ceramic-based artificial stone (whose composition has defied analysis until recently). Cast-iron enjoyed its moment of fashion as the new material in an age which delighted in experimentation.

Long, golden Edwardian afternoons seemed to have characterized the opening decade of the twentieth century, at least in retrospect. The architect Edwin Lutyens designed fabulously detailed and costly houses and gardens for his patrons in styles ranging from what might be termed Surrey Vernacular to the severely Classical.

For the remainder of the century, garden mania developed a leaning towards the instant. Immediate effects responded to the desire for violent visual assault. Walls are painted vibrant blue or purple. Pools, cascades, trees and shrubs are illuminated to dramatize the garden after dark. Even television sets are incorporated into the designs. New plants are bred by plant breeders to gratify the desire for novelty; new devices and gadgets are invented to care for them. And every new feature is obsessively pursued by gardeners driven by age-old habits and desires.

1
Shaping Nature

A Paradise on Earth

All growing and living elements of the garden can be trained, clipped, sheared, pleached, espaliered, cordoned and pruned, or left to grow into an imitation of the wild. Soil can be moved to create patterns and forms, such as amphitheatres or even garden theatres. The more formal the garden the greater the importance and popularity of planting and the shaping of nature in the form of parterres, hedges, topiary, mazes and even living trellis.

The creation of ground-level designs, using evergreen plants, was introduced by the Romans. The Renaissance and Baroque gardens of Italy used box, rosemary and bay in square patterns, embellished with lemon trees in terracotta pots. The parterre reached its finest expression in seventeenth- and eighteenth-century France: miles of dwarf box were formed into geometric and paisley shapes, set against a permanent background of coloured stones and gravel. The French also perfected the clipping of hedges. The gardens of Versailles contained eight million hornbeams trained into seemingly endless hedge around the woodland planting on each side of the main *allées*. The hedges were some-

Opposite Detail of a *parterre de broderie* design from Johann Van Der Groen's *The Netherlandish Gardener* (1699).

times given a spectacularly architectural appearance as colonnades, palissades, arches, columns and whole *cabinets de verdures.*

Opus topiarium was the Roman art of ornamental gardening, of which the clipping of trees and shrubs was only a part. In Roman gardens, hunting scenes or fleets of ships might be cut from cypresses, or even the garden owner's name formed from box. The fashion of clipping evergreens reappeared in the Middle Ages; shrubs might be trimmed into layers like gigantic wedding cakes. The fifteenth-century gardens of the Villa Rucellai in Italy were full of spheres, porticoes, temples, vases, urns, apes, donkeys, oxen, a bear, giants (of both sexes), all formed from various evergreens.

From the seventeenth century, pattern-books were published in the major European countries showing how the adventurous shears-wielding gardener could go about designing and creating his own paradise. All sorts of plants were advocated for the creation of splendid havens of peace. According to one English writer, rosemary was especially popular among women topiarists. The clipping fashion declined in the eighteenth century, to be revived by the Arts and Crafts Movement in the late nineteenth century.

Perhaps the ultimate expressions of planting mania, of the desire to control nature to create a sympathetic and exciting environment, are mazes and labyrinths, which have roots deep in history and legend. In Christian terms they symbolize the soul's journey towards salvation; in their most primitive form mazes were simply traced out on the ground in stones or cut from turf; only later were they delineated by hedges. The gardens of the Villa d'Este boasted no less than four; in 1667 a maze was laid out in the highly symbolic gardens of Versailles around thirty-nine statues representing Aesop's *Fables.*

Perhaps the ultimate expression of the urge to control the planted environment was the turf amphitheatre. All over Europe these were modelled on those in Italian Renaissance gardens, particularly the one in the Boboli Gardens in Florence. The mania for control of the environment thus reached down to the earth itself and to the simplest of plants: grass.

Overleaf A design of the 1660s by Jean Le Pautre
for an elaborate parterre with a central pool and waterjet.

Above The title-page of T. de Bry's *Florilegium*
of 1612, showing an ideal garden.

Opposite Detail of the moated garden of Jakob Trip, Alderman of Amsterdam, *c.* 1700.

Above Plan and bird's-eye view of a *parterre de broderie* garden with a revolving 'Holy Host' fountain from *The Netherlandish Gardener* of 1699. **Preceding pages** A Dutch formal garden *c.* 1700.

Opposite and **above**
Designs from *The Netherlandish Gardener* of knot gardens, planted with herbs and flowers and defined by small hedges of box or yew. and of a maze with a central tree.

Pages 22-23 This print of 1614 evokes the ideal garden of a Dutch couple. symbolic of the good life. **Pages 24-25** Typical Austrian Baroque garden. *c.* 1730: the symmetrical *parterres de broderie* are bordered with sculptures in the antique manner: the shrubs are clipped into the shape of cones and pyramids.

H
B
B
B
E

D
D
B
B
C

Preceding pages Birds-eye view of the château and park at Marly.
c. 1710. built near Paris by Louis XIV.

Opposite A plate from Paul Decker's works (1711) on the palaces of Prussia, where he was Royal Architect.

Above The Italian Baroque gardens of Villa Pamphili near Rome, from Piranesi's *Vedute di Roma* (1740s).

Overleaf John Roque's 1738 view of a party on the bowling green at Claremont, Surrey, England.

Above and **opposite** Two versions of the Baroque garden: the Governor's Palace, Dominica; the Semplici Palace, Cisinello, Italy.

These pages Geometrical forms for clipped shrubs were popular from early Renaissance times. These ideas are from Colonna's *Hypnerotomachia Poliphili,* a philosophical treatise of 1499, in which the garden becomes an emblem for the expression of ideas.

Preceding pages Guiseppe Zocchi's view of the Castel' Pulci in Tuscany as it appeared about 1740.

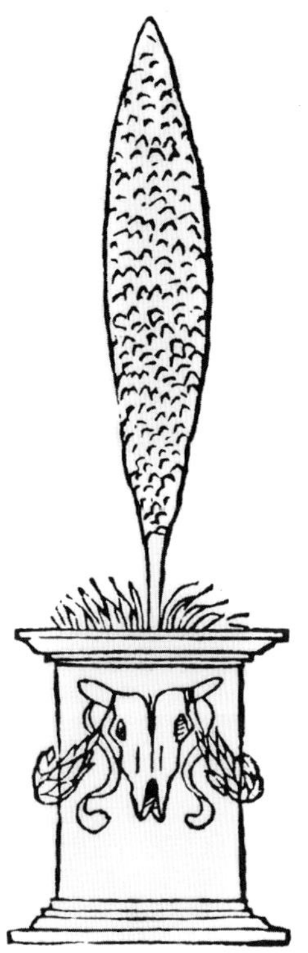

Overleaf Engraving by Nicolaus Visscher
of a late seventeenth-century German garden.

Below A garden from Paul Decker the Elder's early eighteenth-century volume on the palaces and parks near Berlin.

Opposite Part of a Dutch Baroque garden, with grotto, of the same period, recorded by Visscher.

Above A variation on the decorative 'bowling green' popular in the early eighteenth century, in the gardens of the Prince of Schwartzenburg, near Vienna.

Right Salomon Kleiner's view of a sunken 'bowling green', gardens of Count Althan, near Vienna.

Opposite and **below** The renowned hedge labyrinth of the Villa Pisani at Stà: the gardens were designed for the Venetian Doge Alvise Pisani in 1735.

Above A mid eighteenth-century engraving of the renowned turf 'amphitheatre' at Claremont, Surrey, England, *c.* 1725.

Opposite An Arts and Crafts interpretation of a late Renaissance garden by Thomas Mawson.

Preceding pages A proscenium arch of hedge frames a view of the open-air theatre in a Dutch Baroque garden.

Opposite and **above**
Two spectacular avenues:
at Teddesley, seat of Lord
Hatherton, 1840s:
in the Vienna Angarten,
showing the Renaissance
and Baroque style of
clipping limes.

Overleaf A Dutch country-house garden. *c.* 1700.

These pages In the early seventeenth century many exotic and tender plants were imported from the New World. Learned botanical studies were produced with exquisite hand-painted illustrations, and writers gave information on the medicinal uses of the plants, with instructions for their care. These four

kinds of aloes and a flowering cactus, from Abraham Muntinck's treatise, 1666, had probably never been seen before in Europe. Such plants would have been grown in forcing-houses.

Overleaf Empress Maria Theresa's gardens at the Favorita Palace.

Above The famous parterre terraces designed in 1851 by George Kennedy at Bowood, Wiltshire, in E. Adveno Brooke's contemporary watercolour.

Opposite Princely Baroque in the Netherlands: engraving by Nicolaus Visscher, 1709.

Preceding page The parterre gardens at Geubach, Austria.

Overleaf The Baroque water gardens at Geubach, Austria, seat of the Counts Schönborn, 1728; by Salomon Kleiner.

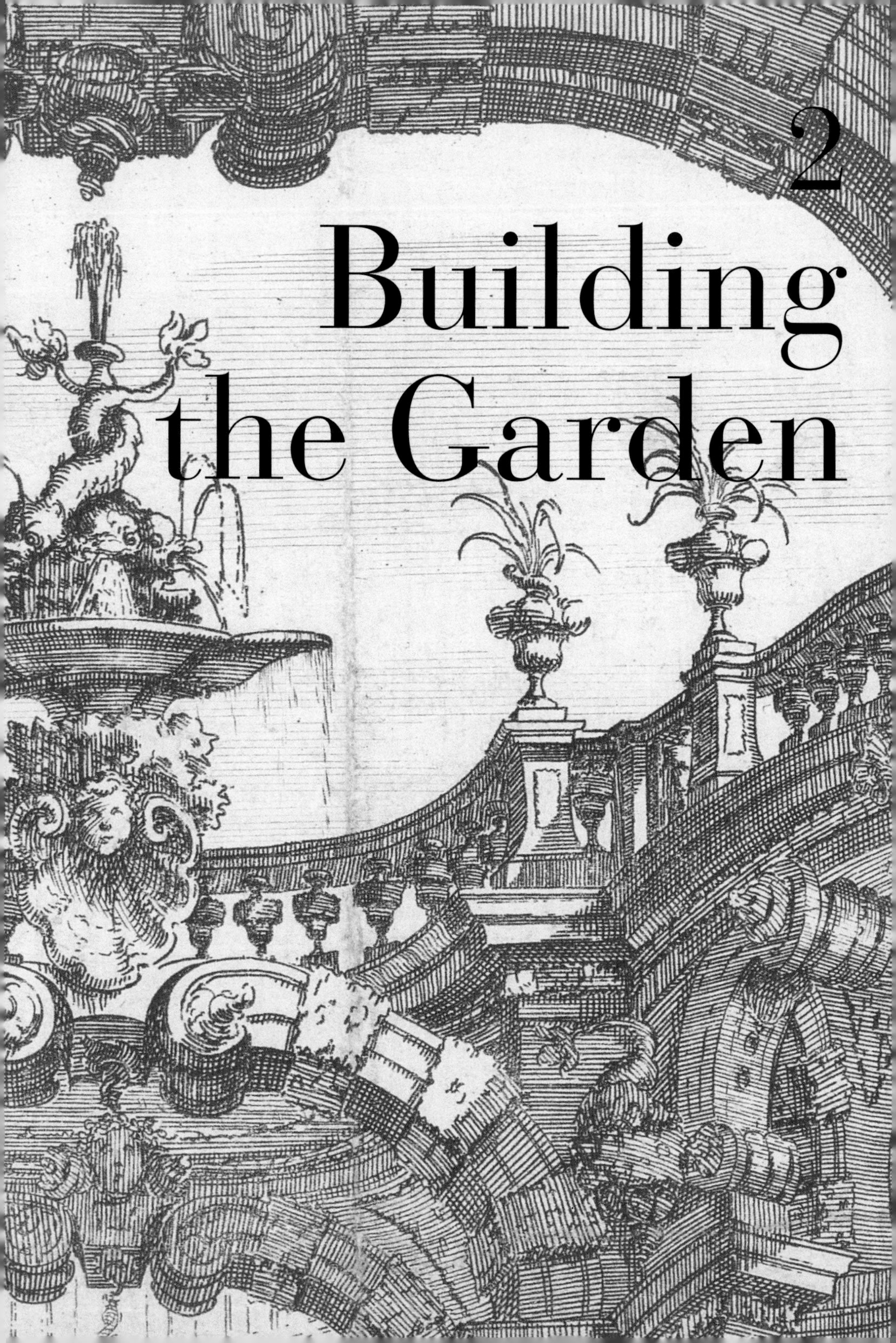

Building the Garden

Temples of Delight

Garden buildings come in every shape, form and style and may serve every conceivable purpose: pavilions to rest in during the heat of the day, temples to draw the eye to the end of a vista, orangeries and conservatories to protect tender citrus plants during the winter and to provide shelter during foul weather, summer-houses for tea, and the family mausoleum, which may have its own special architectural attraction. Horace Walpole remarked of the mausoleum at Castle Howard in Yorkshire that it was enough to tempt one to be buried alive!

Buildings in gardens can make political and social points; at Stowe in Buckinghamshire, Lord Cobham mounted a sustained attack on the government of the day in his Temples of Ancient Virtue, Modern Virtue and British Worthies. They may display the wealth and culture of the owner, refer to the glories of Ancient Rome and the Italian Renaissance, or seek to emulate the extravagance of Versailles. Architecturally, they are often innovative and experimental. Many were never designed to be permanent and were demolished, moved or adapted to the latest whims of fashion

Opposite Detail from a High Baroque garden stage-set by Pietro Righini.

to which they were even more exposed than the house to which they were satellites. A severely classical temple for one generation could be transformed into a rustic grotto for the next. A Chinese house which had formed the central feature of a garden could be removed altogether within decades. For less illustrious patrons, architects like Batty Langley in the first half of the nineteenth century, and William Halfpenny a little later, produced pattern-books illustrating buildings in a delightful range of styles.

Garden architecture is an excellent indicator of prevailing fashions; grottoes, after their long and honourable history dating back to the nymphaeums of classical Rome, vanished without a trace before the wholesome Victorian distaste for damp and draughts. In their place, the summer-house and Swiss cottage became fashionable. The mass-production of glass and cast-iron in the nineteenth century brought a massive expansion in the use of greenhouses and conservatories and speeded the decline of the traditional orangery. Chinoiserie came and went, while the taste for all things Japanese flourished in the context of *fin-de-siècle* styles.

Paradoxically, although the garden is a place where plants normally flourish, it is frequently the buildings which shape and define this earthly paradise. The classicism of Palladio, the self-consciousness of the Picturesque, the real and fake medievalism of abbey, castle or folly, have all left their distinct marks on the spaces which both complement the main habitat and provide a counter-balance to it. Happy the garden owner of the late eighteenth century with a view of a genuine medieval ruin – abbey or castle – such as Fountains or Rievaulx. And if the real was lacking, then the fake would do very well, in the form of towers or hermitages, sometimes with a hermit in residence.

The forms of garden building are myriad: as well as more traditional types, they can include umbrellas, Turkish tents, viewing platforms, kiosks, bath-houses and let us not forget the architecture associated with the modern swimming-pool. As fashions come and go, so the importance of the illustrative print and pattern book becomes apparent, permitting glimpses of past building within the garden enclosure. The elaborate stone loggia of previous generations becomes the timber-decked roof terrace of today.

Above Section through
a garden pavilion near
Antwerp, Belgium, 1827.

Opposite A double-level
Belle Époque pavilion in
a German garden.

These pages Numerous pattern-books were published in the eighteenth century of ideas for garden buildings in every style: here, Gothic, Hindoo, Moorish and Classical.

Preceding pages The 'Fountain of Diana', an Italian Baroque extravaganza, inspired by the gardens of Isola Bella, Lake Maggiore.

Compilations would reproduce ideas and actual designs from architects' own publications, disseminating styles throughout Europe and the colonies.

Garden Building.
Section of Garden Building.

Opposite and **above**
Two Egyptian-style garden
buildings (possibly
mausoleums) with Classical
features, and a section of
a Moorish pavilion, from
the young Sir John Soane's
1797 *Designs in
Architecture*, an inventive
compilation of ideas for
temples and other small
decorative constructions
for the garden.

Overleaf A summer-house interior from Georges
Rémon's *La Décoration Intérieure*, Paris, *c.* 1895.

Opposite Engraving, 1784, of the Gothic Chapel at Strawberry Hill, Twickenham.

Above A mid-eighteenth-century German design for a Baroque garden temple by J.J. Schübler.

Opposite A tower-shaped pavilion with Gothic detailing; a Classical pavilion in the French style; and a domed bathhouse, 1802; the Gothic cottage (*top right*) design by Papworth was published in Ackermann's *Repository*, 1809–28.

Above Design by James Paine, *c.* 1770, for a Classical summer-house done in the Adam style.

Above A rustic 'Banqueting Room' from Charles Over's 1758 album of Gothic and Rococo garden designs.

Opposite Two designs for 'hermitages' from William Wrighte's *Grotesque Architecture, or Rural Amusements,* 1767. This book appeared at the height of the craze for Rococo.

Overleaf The 'Gloriette Chinoise' of the Prince
of Lichtenstein, near Vienna, 1790s.

These pages Four eighteenth-century designs for garden buildings; the larger structures represent examples of Gothic-style pavilions, by Batty Langley (*above*) and by William Halfpenny (*opposite left*). The two Moorish temples *(above and opposite right)* are by Soane, reproduced in Le Rouge's survey of gardens.

Above A plate from Janscha's 1799 volume on the gardens of Hapsburg Austria: here, the Empress Maria Theresa's park at Laxenburg.

Opposite A design by Papworth for a Regency 'Garden Alcove' in Eastern and Chinese styles.

Overleaf The kiosk at Ranelagh, near Paris, from Le Rouge's *Jardins Anglo-Chinois*, 1784.

A Dutch design for a 'rustic chapel' in the Adam style, 1802.

Opposite above Section
of a country house, 1827,
from an album of Dutch
and Belgian design.

Above A German design
for the interior of a 'Chinese
Garden Temple', 1779.

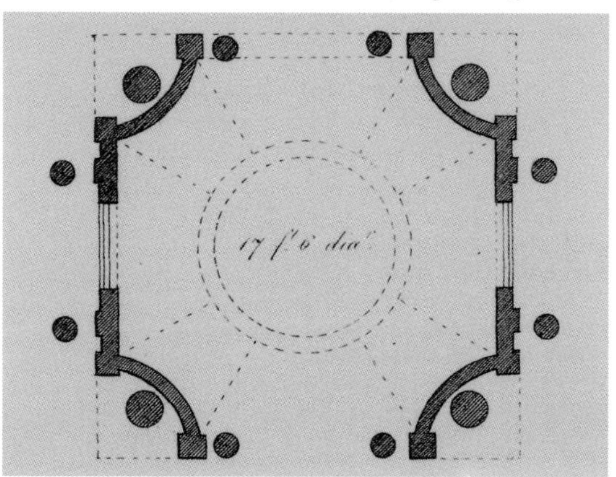

Above and **opposite** Two designs for garden temples from Soane's *Designs in Architecture*, 1778: a cuboid 'Temple for a Flower Garden' in Classical style, and a 'Rusticated Temple' with pillared porticoes.

Overleaf A watercolour of a thatched 'hermitage',
Ackermann's *Repository*, c. 1820.

Opposite and **above** Chinoiserie garden temples from Rococo pattern-books: Paul Decker's of 1759, with a detail: Charles Over's of 1758. Most such designs were too fanciful to be built.

Overleaf Design for an 'Imperial Angling Retreat', from Paul Decker's *Chinese Architecture, Civil and Ornamental*.

Above Baroque pavilions in
the gardens of Prince
Lichtenstein at Rossau.
Opposite Façade of the
'Garden Pleasure House'
at the seat of Count Althan:
from Kleiner's survey of
princely palaces in the
vicinity of Vienna, early
eighteenth century.

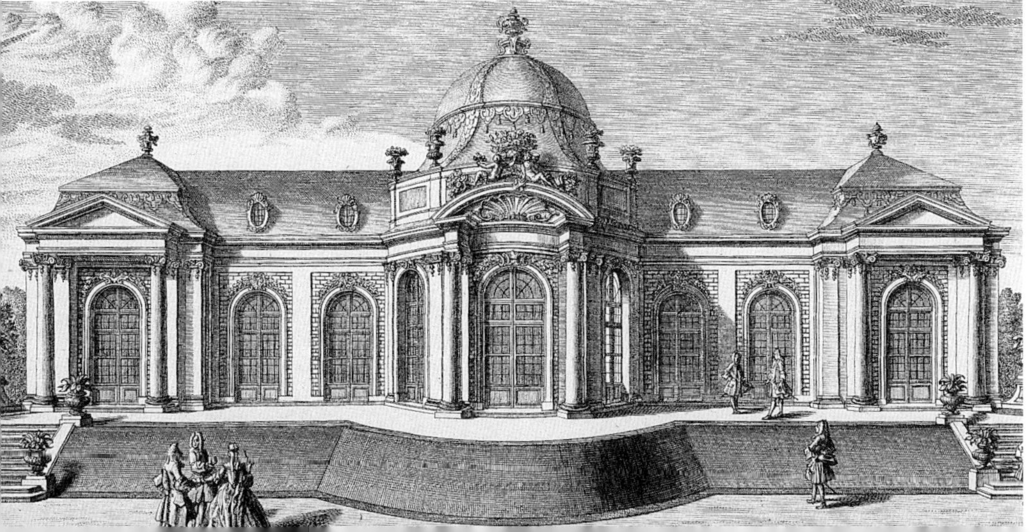

Above A two-storey gardeners' cottage, French, 1855.
Opposite Gardener's house and greenhouse from the same pattern-book.

Overleaf A games room in Beaux-Arts style, Nogent-sur-Mer, northern France, *c*. 1880.

Victor Petit

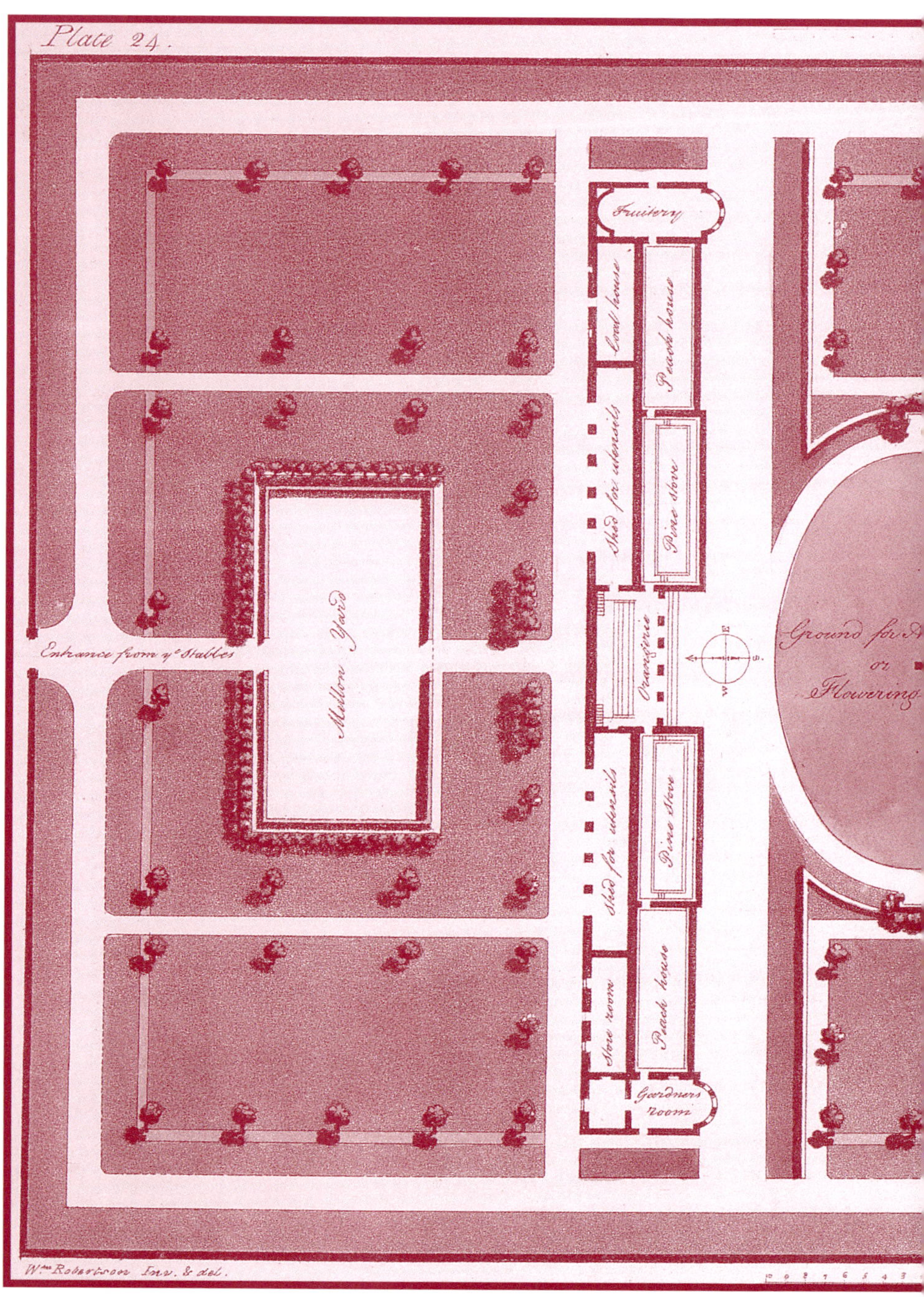

Plan by William Robertson, 1798,
for a range of 'stoves' or hothouses.

110

Overleaf Sezincote, Gloucestershire,
built in 'Hindoo' or Indian style.

Above and **opposite** The winter garden of the Hofburg Palace in Vienna, 1852, richly planted with tender plants and trees, and serving as a popular meeting-place for the local gentry.

Overleaf Designs for Chinese-style pagodas by Le Rouge and by Sir William Chambers, mid eighteenth century.

Tour
près de
Canton.

Above The Chinese-style menagerie from Sir William Chambers' *The Garden and Buildings at Kew*, 1763.

Opposite A carved wooden pavilion in the Gothick taste, from Wallis's *Carpenter's Treasure*, c. 1793.

Preceding pages The Temple of Diana, Erlaw, Austria, with rocky cascade and Chinese bridge, late eighteenth century.

Above A Regency design for a bathhouse, with Greek, Egyptian and Oriental detailing.

Opposite Rusticated Classical façade for a mausoleum, Dutch, 1799.

Overleaf Engraving by Nicolaus Visscher of a Dutch
or German grotto, late seventeenth century.

Above Drawing, 1752, for a 'ruined mausoleum' by Sir William Chambers.

Opposite A 'ruined chapel as hermitage', from a Dutch pattern-book of 1799.

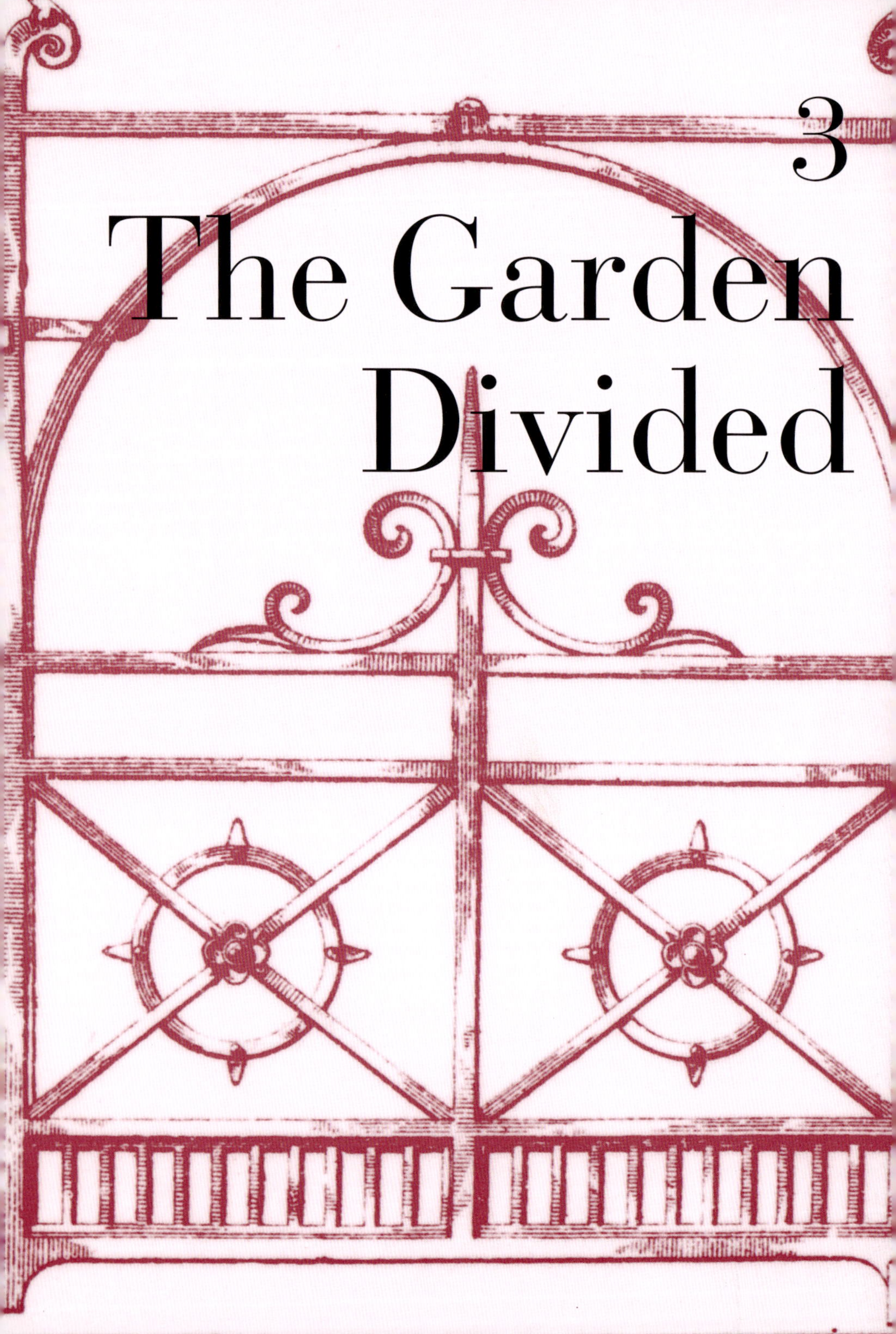

The Garden Divided

Gateways
and Enclosures

The garden is often a place of enclosures within an enclosure; its various parts can be imaginatively linked and divided in a delicious form of horticultural counterpointing. Bridges, terraces, steps, walls and pergolas provide, as it were, an armature for the whole area. In addition to their functional role, many such features are so elaborately conceived and decorated that they can be considered as ornaments in their own right. Bridges, for instance, may serve as crossings of expanses of ornamental water; yet their form, set off by the water itself, is all-important: classical or rustic, arched like Roman bridges, or covered like the wooden ones designed by Palladio in northern Italy. They can be made of wood, stone, brick, or even covered in turf. Bridges frame views or act as foci for the eye. They can be grand and Baroque, or as rustic as a simple plank of wood across a stream. They can be painted a brilliant lacquered red in the Oriental style to brighten up the dullest winter day, or left in their natural wood or stone to blend with their horticultural surroundings.

Opposite Cast-iron balustrading design, late nineteenth-century catalogue from Macfarlane's Castings.

Terraces, steps and staircases are the formal means of dividing and connecting different levels of the garden. By the middle of the seventeenth century monumental stairways and terraces were being put to dramatic use in Italian gardens to emphasize the hill-side sites and, in theatrical manner, to link the architecture of the villa to the natural landscape. The gardens of northern Europe were less disposed to such grand flourishes, but occasionally a steep garden site allowed steps, terraces and balustrades to come into their own. At the beginning of the twentieth century the architect Edwin Lutyens created marvellously well-articulated gardens through the ingenious use of terraces and steps (almost always circular or curved) and other dividing and linking features – walls, alcoves, doorways and pergolas.

The construction of terraces and the steps or ramps to link them has now become prohibitively expensive; no modern gardener can easily undertake the movement of the colossal amounts of earth and rock to create the drama of soaring vertical elevation contrasting with horizontal perspectives of the great multi-level gardens. But we can still relish the art of the balustrade in gardens such as that of Isola Bella on Lake Maggiore. Seen from below, the balustrades delimiting the terraces seem to give the gardens an aerial aspect. And, looking from the gardens, between the cypress trees and decorative urns, they make a division between the finite, enclosed space of the terrace and the infinity of the lake and land beyond. On the subject of balustrades, Sir William Chambers wrote in 1759, 'Such as are intended for use ... must always be nearly of the same height, never exceeding three feet and a half, nor ever being less than three. That is so a person of an ordinary size may, with ease, lean over them, without being in danger of falling.' He realized that the spaces between the balusters were important in relating the enclosed space to the openness beyond.

Yet, other delightful forms of division and opening remain for the present-day gardener. Walls, fences and hedges give privacy and shelter; the materials of their construction, the treatment of their tops, all offer opportunity for ornament and decoration. Gates and gateways – in closed or open work – give a perspective on other parts of the garden or serve to guard their secrets.

Pergolas were originally simple devices to support grape vines. Their decorative possibilities were fully developed by the end of the nineteenth century, until no self-respecting garden was complete without a lengthy run of such structures, with massive cross-beams of green oak supported on alternating square or round pillars. The heaviness of the overall structure was usually offset by cascading swags of rambling roses, clematis and honeysuckle.

The ultimate form of linking (and division, in a sense) has always been the elision of the perceived separation of the formal garden from the natural, semi-tamed lands around. Developed from military architecture, the ha-ha (the obscured sunken ditch) liberated the garden from any walls which limited it and launched it into the surrounding countryside. All Nature had become a garden and a means of return to Eden.

A view of the Chinese
pavilion and bridge, and
the House of Philosophy,
in the Parc de Bonnelles
near Paris, from Le Rouge's
Jardins Anglo-Chinois.

Above and **opposite** Variations on the Chinese bridge in eighteenth-century European gardens, as published by Le Rouge: Windsor, Painshill, and Attichi.

Above The garden at
Stourhead, Wiltshire,
now regarded as the iconic
Picturesque landscape
of Georgian England.

Opposite Even Robert
Adam designed follies: a
'ruined bridge' for Syon
House, engraved by
Vivares, 1768.

Overleaf The bridge across the Dell at Sezincote, Gloucestershire,
the 'Hindoo' house and garden designed by Thomas Daniell.

136

Opposite A design of
1822 for a single-arch
rustic bridge.

Above Chinoiserie bridge
with a central pavilion,
boat and viewing area,
Viennese, 1799.

Preceding pages Designs for garden bridges in Dutch and German pattern-books,
late eighteenth century and early nineteenth.

Opposite Design by French Rococo architect Gilles-Marie Oppenord for a decorated arch.

Above A stagey design of *c.* 1752 for a triumphal arch by Pietro Righini.

Overleaf A massive arch in the winter garden of the Hofburg. the former royal palace in Vienna.

Above 'Arcades for Piazzas',
from Batty Langley's
*Ancient Architecture
Restored and Improved...
in the Gothick Mode*, 1741.

Right 'Head of a Canal
or Termination of a Vista',
from Paul Decker's *Chinese
Architecture, Civil and
Ornamental*.

Overleaf A 'ruined temple with arch' in the gardens of Schönbrunn: from Janscha's 1790s watercolour.

Above A view from the
Upper Terrace at Shrubland,
Suffolk, a painting by
E. Adveno Brook.

Opposite This garden view
of Castle Coombe,Somerset,
also by Brook, combines
several styles – Gothic,
Classical and Baroque.

Preceding pages A seventeenth-century print by Abraham Bosse,
Paris, of a couple carrying blooms from the garden.

Opposite Seventeenth-century designs by Jean Le Pautre of wrought-iron balustrading for garden stairways.

Above The grand staircase at the Villa d'Este, Tivoli, from G.B. Falda's *Le Fontane*, 1675–89.

Overleaf Double stairway linking the upper terrace and the lower gardens of the Belvedere Palace, Vienna, 1720s.

Above and **opposite** German designs of 1775 for friezes; the garden of Jakob Schwind, Mayor of Frankfurt-am-Main, engraved by Merian, 1641.

Above and **opposite** A straight path is the backbone of this formal garden design, *c.* 1900; in contrast, the path in the Picturesque garden winds circuitously.

Above and **opposite** These *treillage* details are from a garden recorded by Paul Decker the Elder, architect to the Prince of Prussia, *c.* 1710; *treillage* would commonly be covered with greenery.

Preceding pages Alton Gardens in Staffordshire, built in the early nineteenth century by the Earl of Shrewsbury.

Below and **right** Even
simple walls may contribute
to aesthetic effect, as shown
in these two German
gardens of the 1820s: a low
wall of open brickwork, and
the battlements of a terrace
belvedere.

Opposite A trelliswork pergola in the form of a tower from a German pattern-book of 1799.

Above A simple trelliswork arcade from *Hypnerotomachia Polifili,* 1499, recalling a medieval garden.

Opposite Humphry Repton's proposal of 1816 for an ironframe semi-circular pergola at Valley Field; fences and shutter gates provide shade.
Above A painted or whitewood single-frame pergola support of the 1850s in the former royal gardens of the Hofburg Palace, Vienna.

Above A pair of cast-iron gates with spear-headed railings opening from a central spine, from an 1890s pattern-book.

Opposite A *clairvoyé*, or see-through screen, in the form of a wrought-iron gateway with grotesque decoration and set in a stonework arch, from Jean Le Pautre's 1660s pattern-book.

Above The gateway of a merchant's country house in the Low Countries, *c.* 1715.

Opposite The garden gates at Strawberry Hill, Horace Walpole's Gothic mansion, begun in 1751.

Overleaf A late nineteenth-century cast-iron gateway for the palace of the Maharajah of Kapurthala, by A. Marcel.

COVPE VVE SVR LE CORP
ECHELLE
ION PRINCIPALE DE LA GRILLE

GARDE
PLAN
GVERITE
CORPS DE

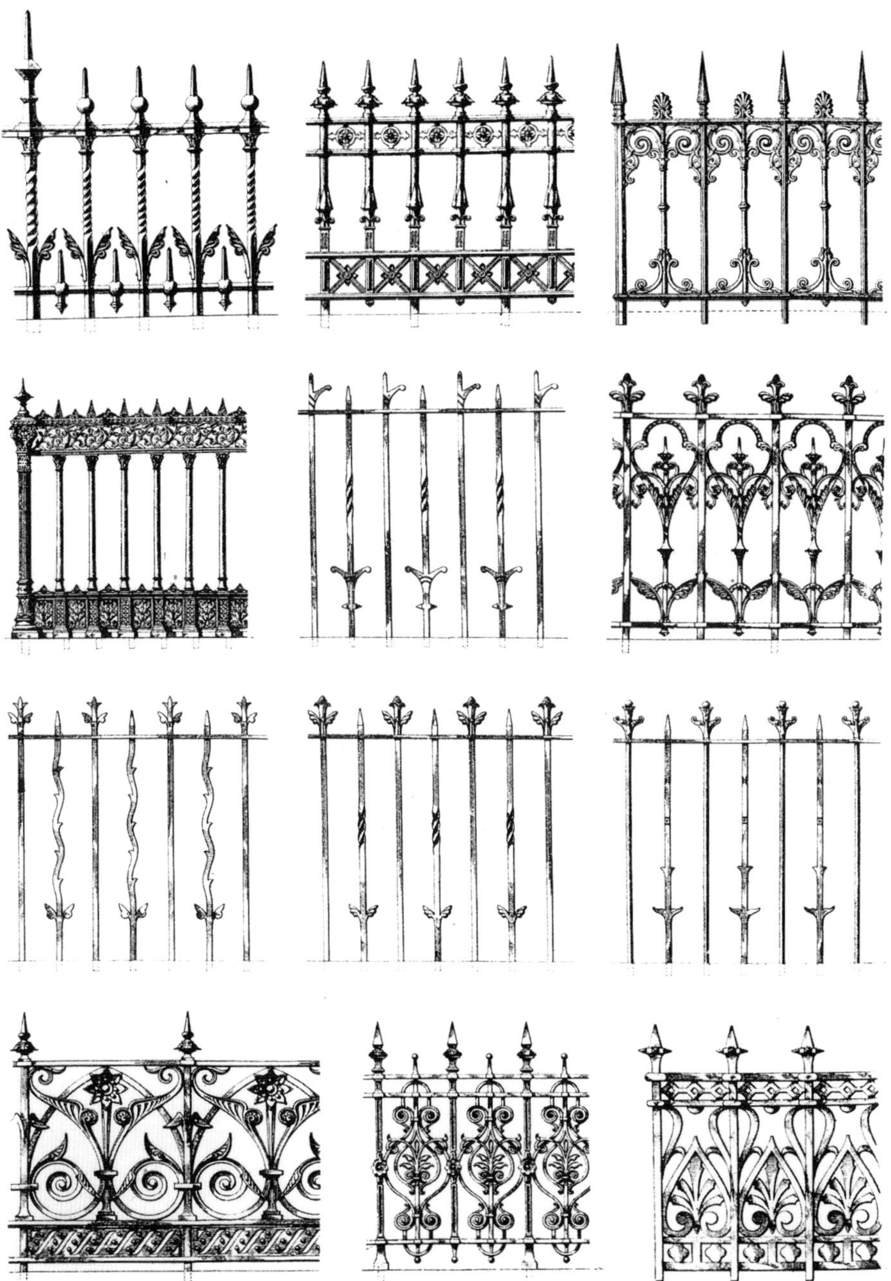

Opposite and **above** Designs for wrought-iron balconies by Jean Le Pautre, 1660s; nineteenth-century designs for cast-iron railings.

The simplest post and paling fence separates this
lodging house from its neighbour. 1825.

LODGINGS
for
SINGLE
MEN

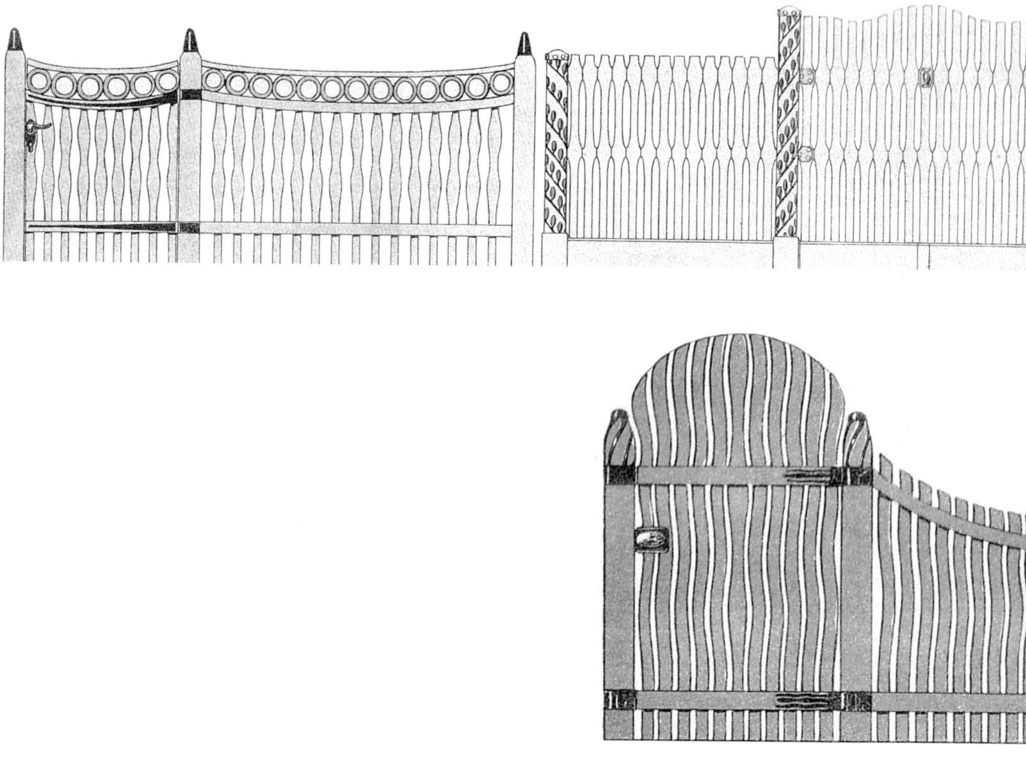

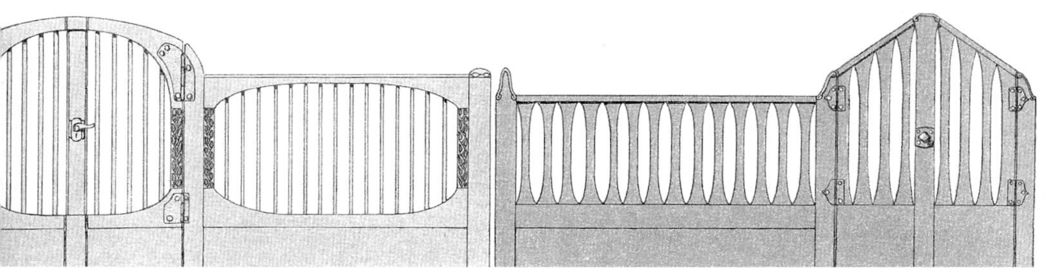

These pages Fences in Jugendstil, the German equivalent of Art Nouveau, by Gertrud Kleinhempel and Otto Bauriedl, published in *Documents: Architecture Moderne*, c. 1905.

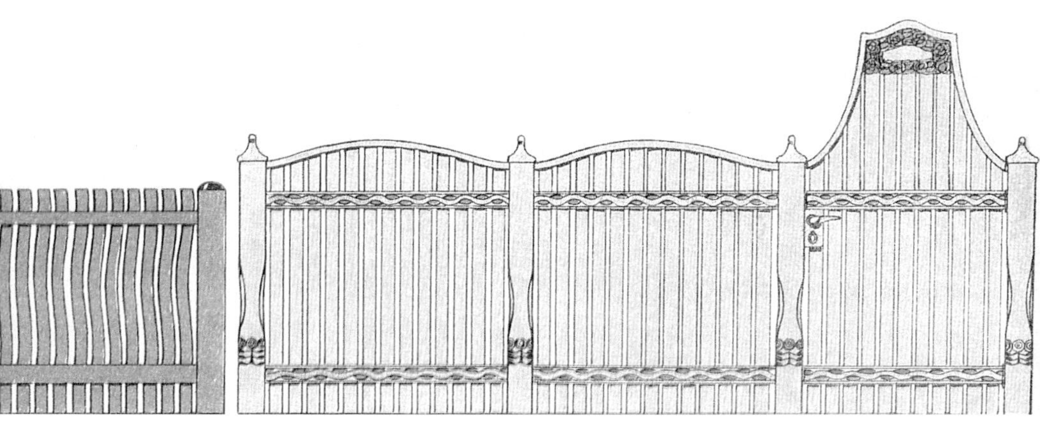

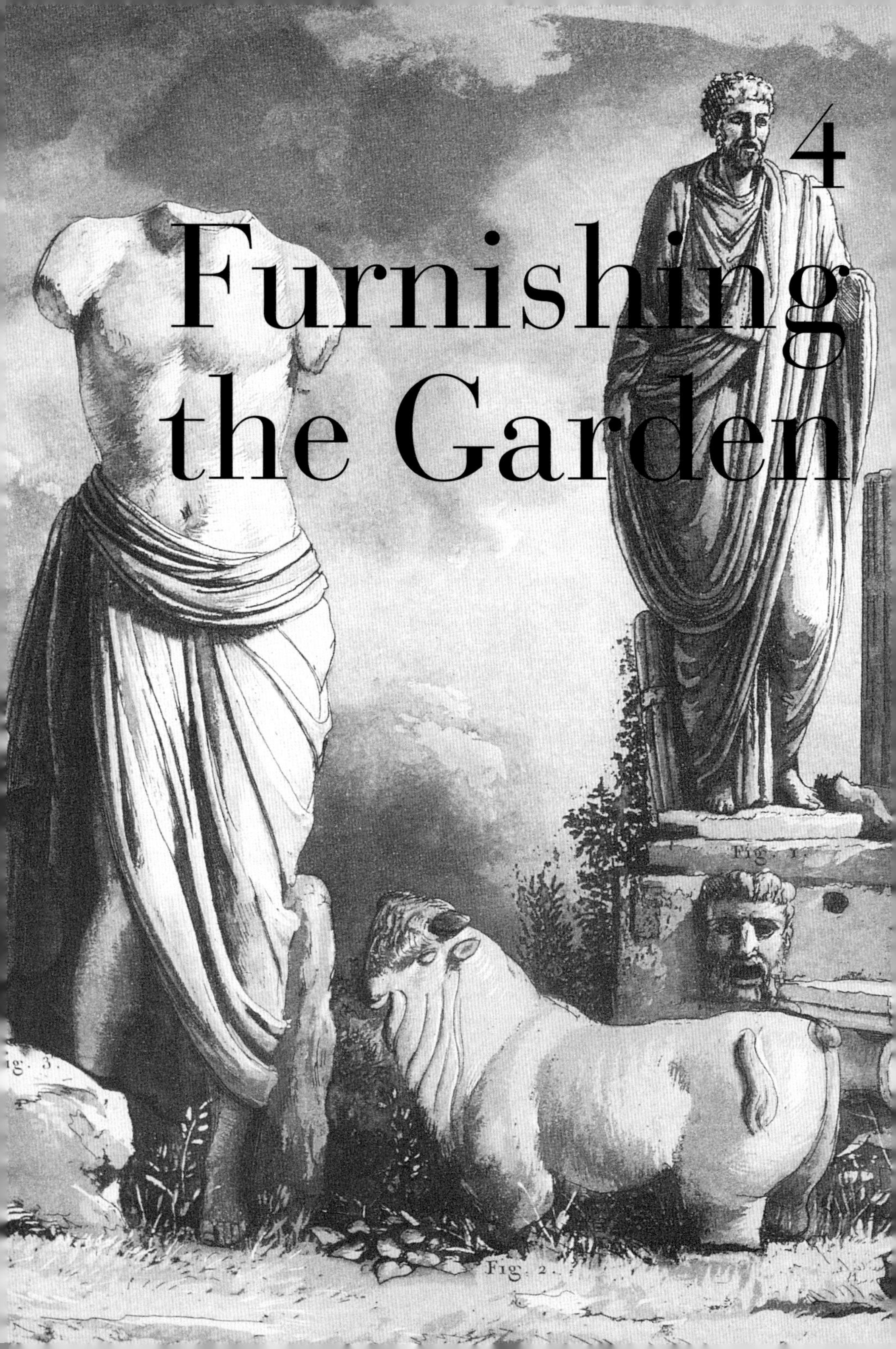

Furnishing the Garden

4

Ornament in Many Materials

Furniture is almost as essential to the fully realized garden as it is to the interior from which the garden is viewed. The setting may be beautiful and the architectural elements impressive, but seats and benches, statuary and urns undoubtedly add a fascinating dimension and embellishment to this paradise on earth. In medieval times, delight was taken in placing fountains in pools, creating turf benches on which to recline, and planting arbours with sweet-smelling climbing plants to give welcome shade on sunny days. Gilded heraldic beasts were placed on green and white striped poles throughout the garden to give a vertical dimension to what might have been an otherwise flat enclosure and, incidentally, to add lustre to a newly enriched family.

During the Renaissance and Baroque periods, the fashion for garden sculpture spread rapidly northwards from Italy, along with Italian craftsmen and architects. Soon, elaborate formal gardens throughout France, Germany and the Netherlands were richly adorned with gods and goddesses, nymphs, satyrs, shepherds,

Opposite Detail of excavated Greek sculpture fragments. *c.* 1813, from J.P.L. Houel's *Landscapes*.

shepherdesses and various beasts of the real and mythological worlds. Hercules, whose labours were reflected in the endless work required to maintain these formal gardens and who represented allegorically the traditional choice between virtue and vice, adorned gardens across Europe, not least in the monumental copy of the Farnese Hercules which dominates the garden at Vaux-le-Vicomte in France. Gilded statues in the gardens at Peterhof outside St. Petersburg catch the rays of the sun and add a golden splendour to the magnificent setting.

At Versailles, apart from the charming set of sculptures illustrating Aesop's *Fables* in the maze, the groups of figures designed by Charles Le Brun reflect the image of Louis XIV as the Sun King. Apollo, the god of the Sun, rises from the waters at the end of the canal. His mother Latona stands surrounded by villagers metamorphosing into frogs, while elsewhere sculptures and fountains reflect the hours, days and seasons as they are governed by the sun.

The materials of garden furniture have always reflected fashion; they have also reflected climate. Marble predominated in Italy, but could not stand the effects of northern winters. Local stone could be harder wearing and cheaper. In England, Portland stone was the most highly prized for sculpture. Cheapest of all materials was lead, sometimes painted in bright colours or made to resemble stone, a sort of poor man's marble. Lead statuary and urns were popular from the late seventeenth century onwards. Gates, railings, seats and benches were usually made of wrought-iron, often with wonderful craftsmanship.

The Industrial Revolution brought new materials to garden ornament. The comparative delicacy of wrought-iron was supplanted by the intricate heaviness of cast-iron, which was cheaper to produce in bulk. The Coalbrookdale and Britannia Ironworks dominated much of international nineteenth-century production, turning out fern-leaved seats and ranges of urns, vases and other sculptural items. The French foundries were noted for their production of animal figures. Bronze, though expensive, is hard-wearing and ideally suited to garden use; it was almost exclusive to the Continent, particularly France. Artificial stone was introduced as a material for garden ornament from the 1760s onwards; stone and then cement were used as the base materials. Mass-produced from moulds, garden ornament spread to a much wider market during the nineteenth and twentieth centuries, as the desire to own a small piece of the classical past spread from grand gardens to much more modest plots.

Above and **opposite** Two examples of circular seats from Charles Over's 1758 pattern-book, *Ornamental Architecture*.

Opposite Two designs by Papworth from *Rural Residences* for tented umbrella seats, of a kind very popular in Regency England.

Above A terminal seat in Classical style from a Dutch pattern-book of 1802.

Preceding pages C.R. Ashbee's designs for green-stained wooden garden terrace furniture in Arts and Crafts style.

Above An ingenious Gothic-style garden building combining a grotto seat for reading and relaxation, with a tented gazebo above.

Opposite Two ladies exchange confidences on a French green-stained garden bench, print by Carmontelle.

Overleaf A selection of chairs and benches for the garden, from William Wrighte's *Grotesque Architecture*, 1768.

Opposite and **above** A classical Mughal garden tent
and two contemporary versions.

Opposite Design by Paul
Decker for a wooden seat
in the Gothic style.

Above French design for a
stone bench with scrollwork
supports set against an
architectural wall, 1880s.

Above Two designs for planters for the conservatory by the Regency cabinet-maker George Smith.

Opposite A nineteenth-century French planter from *Album de l'Industrie et des Arts Utiles*.

Preceding pages Diners on a terrace: a seventeenth-century
print by Moncornet: note the elegant wine-cooler.

Above and **opposite** Two loggias from Jean Boussard's survey of garden buildings in northern France, *c.* 1880: a pavilion on simple pine supports, and a flat-roofed loggia with square column supports.

Preceding pages The 'Rustic Seat' at Shrubland, a famous Italianate Suffolk garden.

Above and **opposite** Variations on the arbour: an Austrian garden shelter of trunks supporting a thatch roof, and a cast-iron arching frame for flowering climbers, designed for Charles Barry's mid-Victorian gardens at Trentham Hall.

Above and **opposite**
Loggia-style summer-
houses in Regency times
ranged from rustic thatched
'cottages' to classical
elegance.

Overleaf A Chinoiserie textile design of an imaginary garden,
with curving pergola and central archway.

Above Bronze urns, from designs for the gardens of Versailles, 1664–89, probably by Claude Ballin.

Opposite A German design, *c.* 1735, of an urn for citrus trees, by Martin Engelbrecht.

Above In the 1820s the
gardens of Wilton were
redesigned in the fashionable
Anglo-Italian manner.

Opposite An Anglo-Italian
style flowering urn in the
terrace gardens at Woburn,
redesigned by Repton
during the Regency.

Above Classic terracotta
pots planted with *cereus
minimus* and *hepatica
trifolia*, painted by G.D.
Ehret, *c.* 1745.

Opposite A clipped bay
tree in a square wooden
tub with ball feet and
finials, still a common sight
on contemporary terraces.

Above A watercolour design by Sir William Chambers for a massive neoclassical urn.

Opposite Three eighteenth-century Dutch designs for garden urns by engraver Simon Schynvoet.

Above and **opposite** Herms would typically be used in Renaissance gardens to line avenues; these examples from an account of Versailles, late 1600s, show Mercury, Minerva, Apollo, and Daphne.

229

Above Detail from
an engraving, *c.* 1729,
of the orange-tree garden
at Chiswick House.

Opposite Frontispiece
to Mondon's volumes of
Rococo designs for garden
architecture, 1736–49,
showing artists at work
in an imaginary ruin.

Overleaf One of Galli da Bibiena's Baroque designs of *c.* 1740
for entertainments and operas in a garden setting.

Opposite and **above** Two colossal statues of satyrs which decorated
the *allées* in the 'wilderness' beyond the *bocage* at Versailles.

Opposite and **above**
Designs for marble sphinxes
mounted by playful gilded
bronze *amours*, or *putti*, on
raised stone bases decorated
with carved swags;
engravings from a volume
on Versailles of the 1690s.

Overleaf Setting for a Baroque opera in a splendid garden filled
with tiers of statues after the antique.

Overleaf The nineteenth-century rose garden at Nuneham Courtney,
with cupid statues on pedestals.

Opposite The frontispiece
from Antoine Le Pautre's
Les Œuvres d'Architecture,
c. 1651.

Above Gentlemen converse,
improbably perched in a
Rococo shell seat on a wall,
design by Jean Mondon.

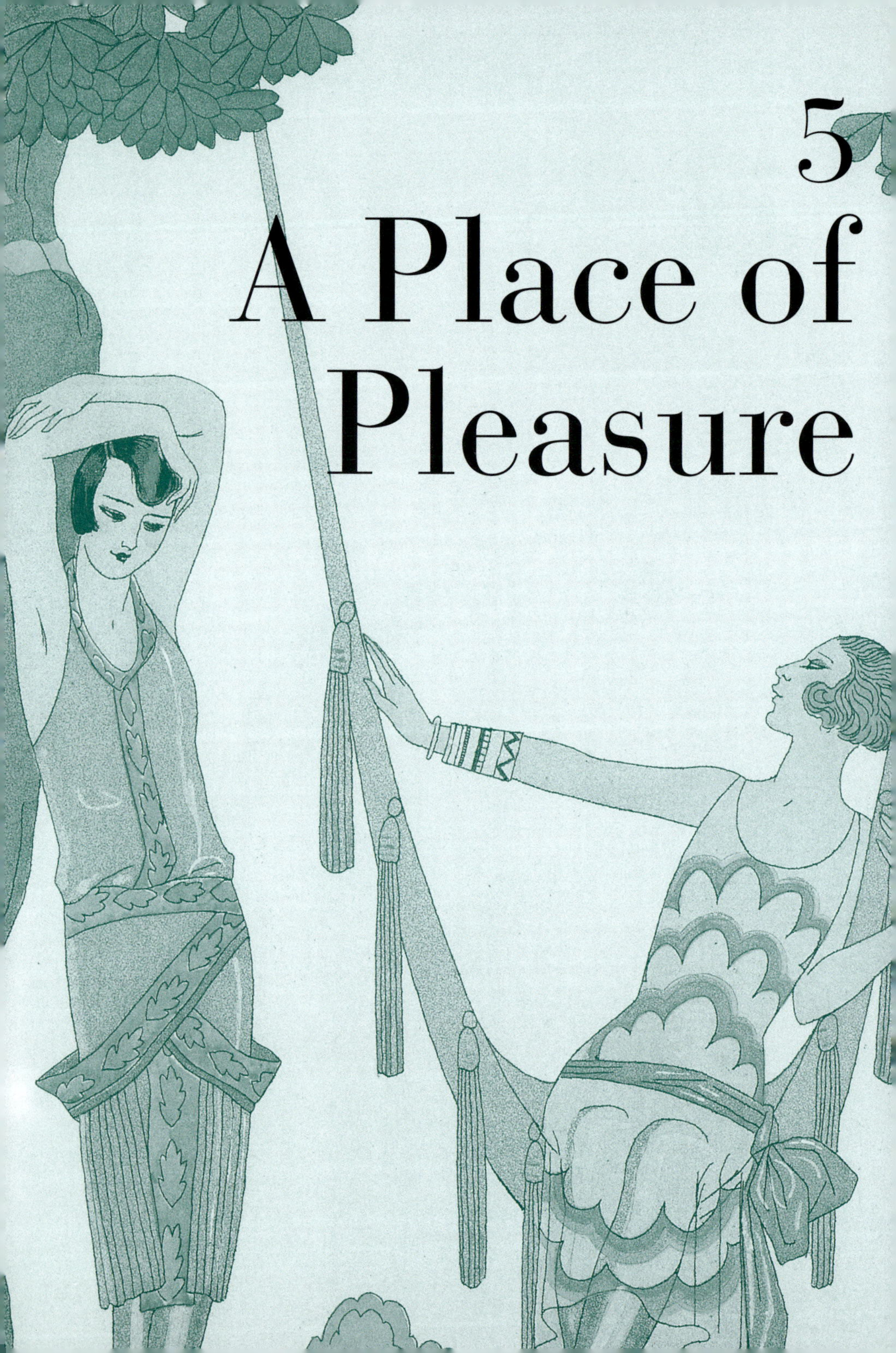

5
A Place of
Pleasure

Amusements and Entertainments

The words 'pleasure garden' may conjure up images of the *louche* night-time delights of Vauxhall Gardens in eighteenth-century London, but pleasure and amusement have often been part of the private garden too. While great cities had vast spaces to entertain the fashionable public with players and orchestras, moonlit concerts, alfresco eating, fireworks and romantic adventures, more secluded and personal places have been enlivened with embellishments simply to delight, from swings and see-saws to the modern swimming-pool. The Chinese pagodas, Turkish tents, Moorish temples and Swiss cottages which were scattered in profusion throughout the gardens at Vauxhall have their equivalent in the tennis-courts of contemporary suburbia.

The spirit of Rococo frivolity in the mid eighteenth century, especially, brought a flavour of casual relaxation to the garden. Devices such as swings and see-saws provided amusement and a measure of sexual *frisson* as billowing skirts revealed momentarily more leg than modesty approved. In France, the gardens at Ram-

Opposite Conversation piece on the garden swing: fashion plate from the *Gazette du Bon Ton*, 1920s.

bouillet were notable for their gigantic and elaborate constructions devoted entirely to play. At Marly, the Duchesse de Bourgogne was famously entertained by 'La Roulette', a gilded toboggan on rails, which the Duchesse and her ladies could ride with happy abandon down a steep incline towards the château. The same spirit of exhilaration made a fashion out of the 'Montagne Russe', or sliding hill; artificial slopes for sledge or toboggan rides had originated in Russia as mounds built out of snow and ice. By the nineteenth century, the helter-skelter had become a standard attraction in fairgrounds and parks.

Formal games, too, have always been an essential part of life in the garden, public and private. *Mail*, an early version of 'golf', was played at Marly in the seventeenth century, while Pall Mall in London acquired its name from the game of *paille-maille*, a form of croquet. Bowling greens were an almost standard feature of seventeenth-century English gardens, and archery remained popular until the nineteenth century.

One of the principal contributions of modern times to the numerous delights of the garden has undoubtedly been the swimming-pool, though garden bathing had been in fashion in earlier times. In the Middle Ages, mixed bathing was a quite acceptable form of relaxation. In later centuries immersion in water came to be regarded with the deepest suspicion; by the eighteenth century, bathing was considered therapeutic, rather than pleasurable. Cold plunges were built in the form of stern, Spartan, stone-edged pools, fed by springs and planted thickly around with evergreens to give year-round shade. The swimming-pool, as we generally know it, is a twentieth-century invention, deriving its popularity originally from the French and, particularly, German cult of sun-bathing in the 1920s. One of the first organically shaped pools was designed by Thomas Church in 1947 at El Novillero, Sonoma, California. Its kidney shape was later much derided as being vulgar and ostentatious, but the architect considered it would integrate more naturally with the flowing natural lines of the garden.

Menageries to house wild animals have been popular since ancient times and were an established feature in Roman gardens. An elaborate example was built at Versailles, in the form of an octagonal pavilion in the centre of an octagonal courtyard, enclosed with wrought-iron screens. It housed birds as well as animals, which included two elephants, camels, ostriches, flamingos and penguins. Fifty years earlier, James I of England had built his own menagerie in St. James's Park. There was also a menagerie in the park of Schönbrunn in Vienna, built in 1752, and another at the Jardin des Plantes in Paris, dating from 1794.

Perhaps the peak of the garden as a place of entertainment was reached at Versailles in the seventeenth and eighteenth centuries, when the park became the setting for entertainments and fêtes to mark gala occasions. In Louis XIV's reign plays and masques by Molière and Racine, with music composed by Lully, were performed in temporary theatres that encompassed large areas of garden. The canal was illuminated and ships and palaces floated on it, while make-believe monsters rose from the depths. The garden theatre of the Sun King, as a place of celebration and frivolity, has never really been surpassed.

Above The swing at Rambouillet, near Paris, operated by ropes and pulleys.

Opposite A somewhat nervous lady in a chair swing, early nineteenth-century French fashion print by Delacourt.

Above A chair swing beneath a cherry tree, *c.* 1810, from the *Bon Genre* series.

Opposite A very basic swing, from a French fashion plate of the 1920s.

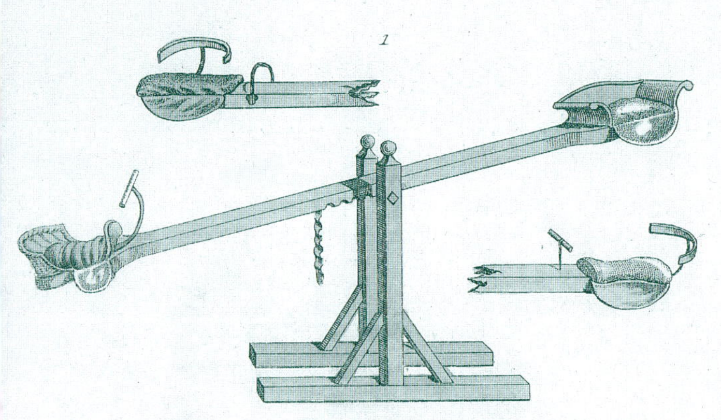

Above A wooden see-saw, from a Dutch pattern-book of 1802.

Below Designs for swings on arch frames from the same book.

Opposite A swinging seat beneath a 'Chinese' tent roof, 1799.

Overleaf An early nineteenth-century print after L. Garneray of the 'Montagne Russe' (Russian Mountain), a helter-skelter in a Paris park.

Above A German design, *c.* 1800, for a miniature carousel or whirligig with bucket seats for two girls and cantilevered extensions for more adventurous boys. **Opposite** A basic wood-frame ferris wheel with wicker-work seats, worked by pulleys on a wheel and ratchet system, *c.* 1800.

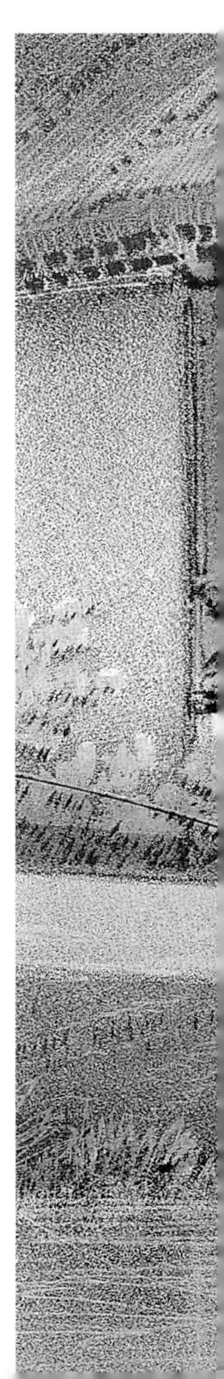

Opposite A belvedere with deck surround and steps attached.
Below A thatched open-fronted arbour shelter; both examples are from Victor Petit's *Habitations Champêtres*, c. 1855.

Above and **opposite** Two designs for rustic pavilions beside water by Victor Petit: one shelter serves as boathouse and landing stage, while the half-timbered pavilion with a six-gabled roof makes an attractive belvedere.

Above High Rococo – the boating lake facing the 'Egyptian' belvedere at Steinfort, as published by Le Rouge, with chain ferry in Chinese style and a 'Cantonese' junk. **Opposite** A gondola-style punt with a Chinese canopy.

Above The swimming habit from the *Gazette du Bon Ton*, 1913.

Opposite A convenient topiary half-*clairvoyé* provides a glimpse of these flappers' summer dip, from *Galérie des Modes*, 1920s.

Above and **opposite** Renaissance and Baroque garden designers often provided amusements in the form of joke fountains; typically, water would spurt forth to soak the passer-by, activated by foot pressure or other devices: these two examples are from Falda's *Le Fontane*.

Overleaf A party from a riverside house takes to the ice in a horse-drawn gondola sleigh, engraving by Lannesin after Watteau's *Winter*.

266

A boy guides his sleigh with his brother and their nurse, early eighteenth-century German print.

Above Thomas Mawson designed this 1909 cricket pavilion for Thornton Manor in Westmoreland.

Opposite Pavilions for the practice firing-ranges built at La Favorita, a royal palace near Vienna, recorded by Salomon Kleiner, 1720s.

Above Garden skittles, from a German pattern-book of 1799; framework and enclosure are in Gothic style.

Opposite An ornamental swing slung between two sculpted figures, in high Rococo Chinoiserie style, from Le Rouge's *Jardins Anglo-Chinois*.

Above and **opposite**
Observatories in the form
of belvederes and gazebos
embellished many a well-
furnished eighteenth- and
nineteenth-century garden:
two fine 1850s examples
from France in Victor
Petit's rustic manner.

Overleaf A mid-eighteenth-century group scans the surrounding countryside
with a telescope, while gentlemen try their luck in the fishpond.

Above A gazebo with a stairway in its central column offers views of the lake in the park of St. Denis, Paris, 1880s.

Opposite A French hostess waves from her terrace; a plate from the *Gazette du Bon Ton*, 1913.

Overleaf A garden building in the bastion walls of a French country house; the doors below give access to steam baths, from Boussard's survey, *c.* 1880.

MACHINE · VAPEUR

Above and **opposite** Plates from the *Gazette du Bon Ton* showing guests at a private entertainment, and a woman descending a flight of steps into the garden – to keep a tryst?

Overleaf A night-time entertainment amid the *treillage* of the Salon
at Versailles in the reign of the Sun King.

6

Water

The Most Vital Element

Water brings life to gardens; without it, all plants would die. Yet water is more than just sustenance: its flash and sparkle as it falls in a cascade or its chatter as it runs down a hill or staircase delights the eye and soothes the ear. Water in the garden has the property to exhilarate, even to alarm, but it may also bring peace and inward calm. From the very earliest times gardeners have manipulated the element to achieve a myriad of effects.

Moving water excites: fountains, rills and cascades all raise the spirits. These special qualities were fully understood by the designers of Mughal and Islamic gardens. Water chutes of carved and fretted marble were angled to catch the sun, creating a reflection from the sparkling water as it fell from one terrace to another. At night-time, candles were placed behind cascades to give glittering illumination. In Italy, the water which pours from the Oval Fountain at the Villa d'Este delights in its richness and complexity, while at Caserta the onlooker is overawed by the monumental cascade which runs towards the palace. The French designers and gardeners of Versailles and Vaux-le-Vicomte made sure that their magnificent fountains were overwhelming in their number and

Opposite Detail of the Baroque fountain of Pluto and Proserpina at the Belevedere Palace, Austria.

variety. And in the great gardens of Peterhof, near St. Petersburg, the water cascades into marble basins and is then shot skywards from gilded figures, before running into a canal which stretches towards the Gulf of Finland in the distance.

The mechanical properties of water have also been harnessed to enliven the garden. In the great Baroque gardens of Italy hydraulic pressure activated automata to surprise and alarm — birds sang, organs played and concealed jets soaked the unwary guest. In more modern times water has been used to create screens to conceal bathers in swimming pools or to veil sculptures, a device inspired by Indian Mughal gardens.

Still water is calming and refreshing. Islamic gardens contained tanks of water, full to the brim to reflect the surrounding architectural glories. Gertrude Jekyll, the great Arts and Crafts gardener, was influenced by memories of the Alhambra; Sir Edwin Lutyens created Moorish tanks with covered walks on two sides. At Versailles, the Parterre d'Eau immediately outside the garden front of the palace is composed of two large mirrors of water in which the elaborate façade of the palace is reflected. The canals of so many Dutch and Dutch-inspired gardens have the same effect of inducing feelings of peace and tranquillity.

Water in movement and standing water were combined with marvellous ingenuity in the gardens of the English Landscape Movement of the eighteenth century. Natural-seeming lakes were created over several acres; reflected in their still waters might be a temple or an urn on an island, or perhaps a grotto. The water could then be directed to plunge over a spectacular cascade into a further lake, creating drama and excitement to equal that of the most architectural Italian garden. At Chatsworth, in Derbyshire, the canal to the south of the house, dug at the command of the first Duke of Devonshire when he decided to have a hill which blocked his view removed, reflects the house, which seems to rise up from the mirror of the water. And, then, water in dramatic movements erupts, as a gardener opens a valve with a giant key and the jet from the Emperor Fountain rises thirty metres into the air. The image in the mirror is shattered.

LES III. FONTAINES

Opposite The fountains at Versailles were Louis XIV's favourite feature: Dominic Girard, author of this 1714 engraving, was chief fountain engineer. **Above** The 'Spirit of Valour', centrepiece of a Versailles fountain, *c.* 1670.

Above and **opposite** Two engravings of *rocaille* Cupid fountains from the series of 1670s volumes on Versailles: scallop shells. cupids. dolphins. and lyres were favourite motifs of the period.

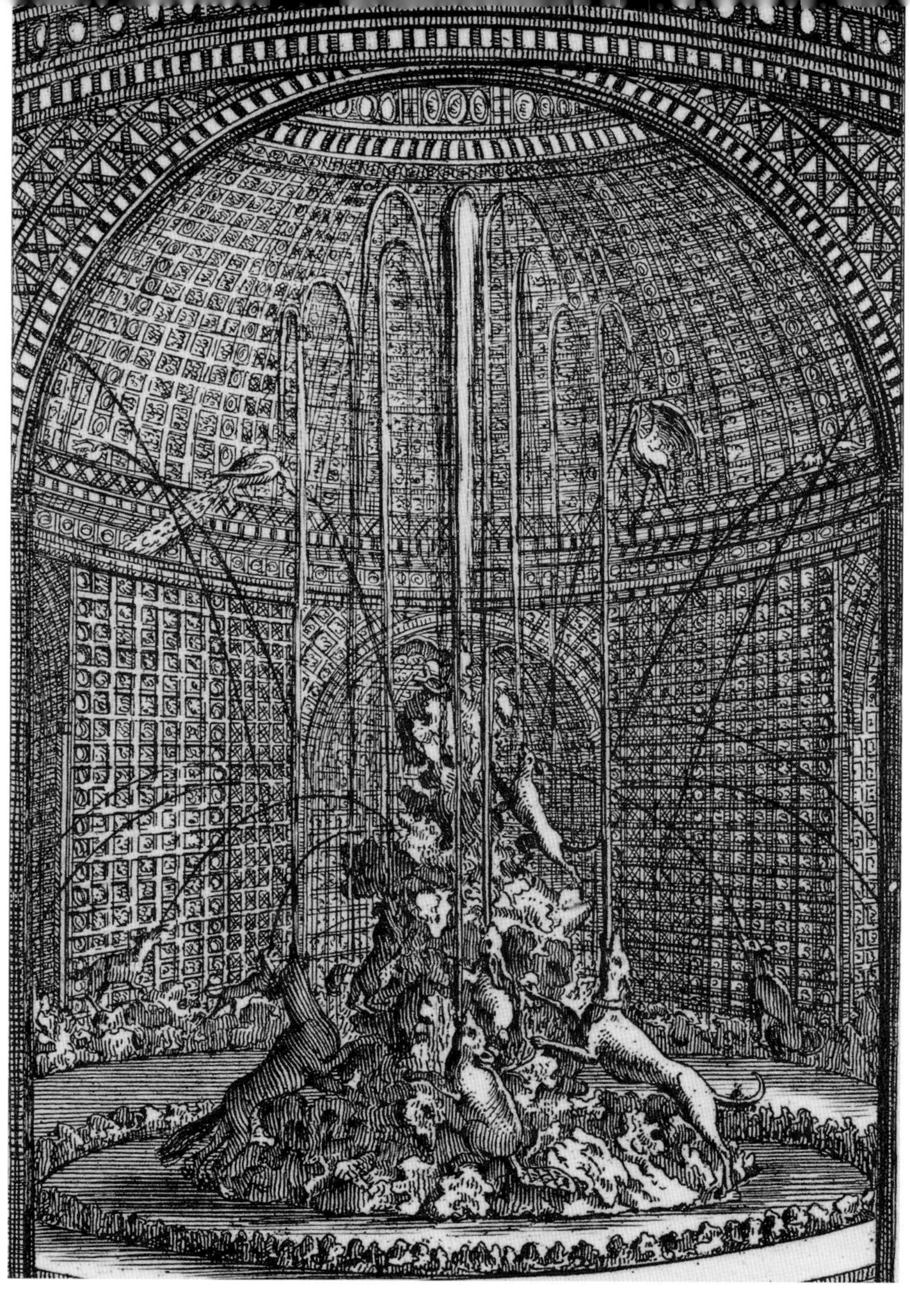

Above and **opposite** The labyrinth of *bocage* with *treillage* arbours at Versailles was ornamented with small fountains on the theme of Aesop's *Fables*; in 1770 these were recorded by Daniel Bellamy Snr. in his volume of *Ethic Amusements*.

Above left Detail of the Fountain of Venus at Versailles, by Girard.

Above right A Rococo fountain design by Jean Mondon the Younger.

Opposite Design for a Baroque fountain in the 'Italian style' by Jean Le Pautre, Paris, *c.* 1661.

Preceding pages The double Terrace of One Hundred Fountains cuts across the main axis of the Villa d'Este, Tivoli, from Falda's *Le Fontane*.

300

The circular lake at
Versailles was a popular
meeting-place for the
courtiers of Louis XV.

Above and **opposite** Sea gods and aquatic creatures – strange fish and dolphins – were common motifs in fountain design in both the 17th and 18th centuries; the fashion started in the Baroque period.

B
A
C
D

Opposite Three designs for revolving fountains, to be set in the centre of a pool, from *The Netherlandish Gardener*, 1699.

Above The goddess Arethusa in an ideal garden. *c.* 1736.

Overleaf The 'Rustic Fountain' on the cascade at the Villa Aldobrandini, Frascati, from Falda's *Le Fontane*.

APPARTEMENS VERTS ET
Font. d'Arethuse

PARTIE HAUTE DE LA RIVIERE.

PARTIE BASSE DE LA RIVIERE.

Overleaf The symbolic channelling of water in the Islamic garden; engraving of Babar's Tomb, Atkinson's *Afghanistan*, 1842.

Below and **opposite** Two cascades by D. Girard for Le Nôtre's 'theatre of water' at Versailles; the Great Cascade was set in an amphitheatre.